Mighty Lions

Charlotte Guillain

Raintree is an imprint of Capstone Global Library Limited, a company incorporated in England and Wales having its registered office at 7 Pilgrim Street, London, EC4V 6LB – Registered company number: 6695582

www.raintreepublishers.co.uk
myorders@raintreepublishers.co.uk

Text © Capstone Global Library Limited 2013
First published in hardback in 2013
Paperback edition first published in 2014
The moral rights of the proprietor have been asserted.

Edited by Daniel Nunn, Rebecca Rissman, and Catherine Veitch
Designed by Victoria Allen
Picture research by Mica Brancic
Production by Victoria Fitzgerald
Originated by Capstone Global Library Ltd
Printed and bound in China by CTPS

ISBN 978 1 406 26077 9 (hardback)
17 16 15 14 13
10 9 8 7 6 5 4 3 2 1

ISBN 978 1 406 26084 7 (paperback)
18 17 16 15 14
10 9 8 7 6 5 4 3 2 1

British Library Cataloguing in Publication Data
Guillain, Charlotte.
Mighty lions. -- (Walk on the wild side)
599.7'57-dc23
A full catalogue record for this book is available from the British Library.

Acknowledgements
We would like to thank the following for permission to reproduce photographs:Alamy p. 16 (© Design Pics Inc./Carson Ganci); Corbis p. 25 (© DLILLC); Getty Images pp. 4 (PhotoDisc), 13 (Panthera Productions), 26 (Oxford Scientific/Owen Newman), 17 (Flickr/Giles Breton); Nature Picture Library pp. 5, 9, 11, 29 (all © Andy Rouse), 7 (© Suzi Eszterhas), 10, 12, 15, 19, 20, 22, 28 (all © Anup Shah), 14 (© Inaki Relanzon), 18(© Philippe Clement), 21 (© Laurent Geslin), 23, 27 (both © Tony Heald); Shutterstock pp. 8 (© Keith Levit), 24 (© Villiers Steyn).

Cover photograph of an African lion reproduced with permission of Nature Picture Library (© Andy Rouse).

We would like to thank Michael Bright for his invaluable help in the preparation of this book.

Every effort has been made to contact copyright holders of material reproduced in this book. Any omissions will be rectified in subsequent printings if notice is given to the publisher.

All the Internet addresses (URLs) given in this book were valid at the time of going to press. However, due to the dynamic nature of the Internet, some addresses may have changed, or sites may have changed or ceased to exist since publication. While the author and publisher regret any inconvenience this may cause readers, no responsibility for any such changes can be accepted by either the author or the publisher.

Some words are shown in bold, **like this**. You can find out what they mean by looking in the glossary.

Contents

Introducing lions .4

Where do lions live? 6

What do lions look like? 8

Camouflage 10

Pride life 12

Caring for cubs 14

Night work 16

Hunting 18

Eating 20

Territory 22

Lion talk 24

Resting 26

Life for a lion .28

Glossary 30

Find out more 31

Index 32

Introducing lions

Lions are beautiful, powerful **carnivores**. They are part of the cat family, but they are very different to pet cats! Lions are part of a group called big cats. Tigers, leopards, and cheetahs are also big cats.

leopard

lion

Where do lions live?

Most lions live in Africa, but a small number also live in western India. An African lion's main **habitat** is a grassy plain, called the **savannah**.

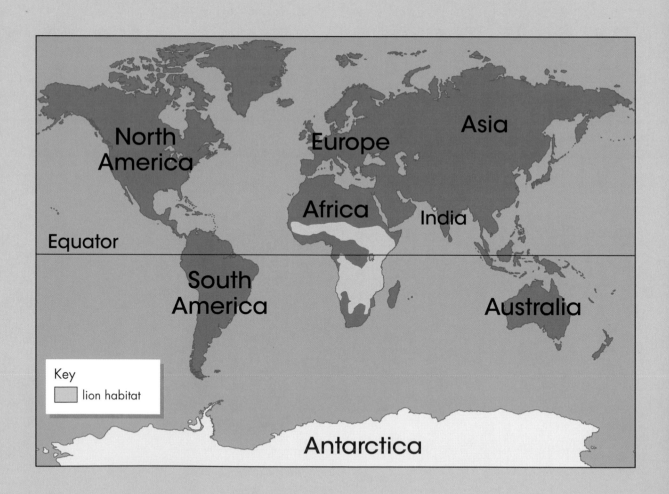

North America

Europe

Asia

Africa

India

Equator

South America

Australia

Key

lion habitat

Antarctica

Lions live in many African countries.

What do lions look like?

Lions are large and strong. They have powerful muscles in their legs to help them catch and hold **prey**. A male lion's mane makes it look bigger and can protect it in a fight.

Did you know?

Male lions are the only cats to grow manes.

Female lions, or lionesses, are smaller than male lions.

9

Camouflage

Lions' fur is a yellow-brown colour. It blends in with the dry grass on the **savannah**. When lions hunt, they **stalk prey** slowly through the grass. The prey can't see the lions until they start to run.

Lions' fur is a great **camouflage** when they hide in the long grass.

Pride life

Lions live in groups called **prides**. Most lions in a pride are female. Lionesses stay with their mothers when they grow up. A few males also live in the pride. The males protect the pride from **predators** and from other male lions.

Did you know?

In each pride there can be 10 to 40 lions.

Caring for Cubs

The lionesses in a **pride** often have their **cubs** at the same time. Newborn cubs have spotted fur. The lionesses in a pride help to look after each other's cubs. They feed and protect any cub, not just their own.

Mother lions teach their cubs how to hunt.

Night work

Lions are most active at night and rest during the day when the sun is very hot. Lions can see very well in the dark. Their strong senses of smell and hearing help them to find **prey**.

Lions can sneak up on their prey more easily in the dark.

Hunting

In a **pride**, the lionesses do most of the hunting. Sometimes they work as a team, creeping close to a herd of **prey**, such as zebra or antelope. When the lionesses are close enough, they run at the prey and pounce. They kill the animal by biting its throat.

Eating

Lions only eat meat. When lions kill **prey**, they share it with the rest of the **pride**. The lions in a pride fight each other to get the most meat. Male lions usually eat before the lionesses. **Cubs** eat what is left of the food at the end.

Did you know?
Lions usually eat every three or four days.

Territory

A **pride** of lions has its own **territory**. This is an area of land that provides the food and water that the pride needs. Lions guard their territory to stop other **predators** hunting there. This makes sure there is plenty of food and water for the pride.

Lions mark their territory with **urine** to keep other prides out.

Lion talk

Lions roar to warn other **prides** of lions to keep out of their **territory**. Lions in a pride greet each other by rubbing heads or licking each other.

Lions can roar louder than any other big cat.

Did you know?

A lion's roar can be heard 8 kilometres away.

Resting

Lions use a lot of energy when they hunt so they need to spend a lot of time resting. Sleeping helps lions to save energy ready for the next hunt.

Lions can spend around 20 hours a day resting.

Did you know?

When male lions have eaten a big meal, they can rest for days.

Life for a lion

Lions are fearsome hunters with terrifying roars. But they work as a team and look after each other. Sadly, lions' **habitats** are getting smaller and there is less **prey** for them to hunt. Humans need to protect this great animal and help it to survive.

A lioness doesn't hurt her **cub** as she carries it in her mouth.

Glossary

camouflage colouring or disguise that hides an animal from view

carnivore meat-eater

cub baby lion

habitat natural home for an animal or plant

predator hunts other animals for food

prey animal killed by another animal for food

pride group of lions

savannah area of grassland found in many parts of Africa south of the Sahara Desert

stalk creep up on

territory area of land where one animal or group of animals lives

urine wee

Find out more

Books

African Cats, Keith Scholey & Amanda Barrett (Disney Editions, 2011)

Face to Face with Lions, Dereck Joubert (National Geographic, 2008)

Fierce Lion, Tom Jackson (Wayland, 2011)

Killer Cats, Alex Woolf (Franklin Watts, 2011)

Lion vs. Gazelle, Mary Meinking (Raintree, 2012)

Websites

gowild.wwf.org.uk/regions/africa-fact-files/african-lion
The World Wildlife Fund website has a fact file on lions.

kids.nationalgeographic.com/kids/animals/creaturefeature/lion/
This National Geographic website has information on many animals, including lions.

Index

big cats 4

camouflage 10, 30
carnivores 4, 30
cheetahs 4
cubs 14, 20, 30

eyesight 16

fighting 8, 20
fur 10, 14

greetings 24

habitats 6–7, 28, 30
hearing 16
hunting 10, 14, 18–19, 26

leopards 4
lionesses 9, 12, 14, 19, 20

male lions 8, 12, 20, 27
manes 8
muscles 8

predators 12, 22, 30
prey 8, 10, 16, 17, 18, 20, 28, 30
prides 12–13, 14, 18, 20, 22, 23, 24, 30

resting 16, 26–27
roaring 24, 25

savannah 6, 10, 30
senses 16
size 8, 9
smell, sense of 16
stalking 10, 17, 18, 30

teamwork 18, 28
territory 22–23, 24, 30